"I AM"s
OF JESUS IN THE BOOK OF JOHN

A Study by Jeff Archer

ONE STONE
BIBLICAL RESOURCES

Published by:
One Stone Press
979 Lovers Lane
Bowling Green, KY 42103

Printed in the United States of America

ISBN 10: 1-941422-19-5
ISBN 13: 978-1-941422-19-9

Supplemental Materials Available:

➢ Answer Key

➢ Downloadable PDF

www.onestone.com

ONE STONE
BIBLICAL RESOURCES

CONTENTS

I AM
WHO I AM

Before looking at the statements/claims of Jesus in the New Testament, let's examine an Old Testament statement made by God. Perhaps when one reads "God" in the Old Testament, his mind automatically thinks of God the Father. However, when one reads the term "God," it may also refer to God the Son or God the Holy Spirit. Each person in the Godhead is "God" and possesses the attributes of the Divine Nature. So, as one examines this term "I AM," he should not exclusively think of the Father, but also of Jesus and the Holy Spirit.

1. God speaks to Abraham in Genesis 12:1ff, but the Bible does not tell us what term Abraham uses to refer to God. In Genesis 17:1, how does God introduce Himself?

   _____

The Bible uses the term "mighty" to describe God and man. It uses the word "Almighty" only in reference to God. Job and his friends, who probably lived around the same time as Abraham, use this term 31 times. It is used 48 times altogether in the Old Testament. In the New Testament, it is used ten times: once in 2 Corinthians 6:18 in a quote from an Old Testament prophet and nine times in Revelation. In Revelation 19:6 (in the KJV and NKJV), the term is translated "Omnipotent." It is translated "Almighty" all other times.

2. What does the combination of terms, God Almighty, emphasize about the character/ attributes of God and why is this important for Abraham to know (Gen. 17:1-8)?

   _____

3. By what term is God known to Abraham, Isaac and Jacob and what term do they not know (Exo. 6:3)? _____

4. By what term does God want the children of Israel to know Him (Exo. 6:7)? _____

   _____

5. When Moses encounters God on Mount Horeb, how does God introduce Himself (Exo. 3:6)? _____

   A. Why is this identification important to Moses? _____

   _____

6. God tells Moses He is sending him to Egypt to deliver His people Israel; what question does Moses say the children of Israel would ask (Exo. 3:13)? _____

_____

7. What is God's answer (Exo. 3:14)? _____

_____

8. What connection does God make with their past to help the children of Israel understand Who He is (Exo. 3:15-17)? _____

_____

Note: the term "God" is from the Hebrew word Elohim. It is used 2,601 times in the Old Testament. "El" (means God) and "him" (makes the word plural) was used of the true God, false gods and judges. The term "LORD" is from the Hebrew word YHWH. It is used 6,521 times in the Old Testament. The Bible only uses this term to refer to the true God. Some translations (KJV, NKJV, NIV, and NASB) use the word "LORD" (all caps) to translate this term. The ASV uses the word "Jehovah" to translate this term.

9. What does the term "LORD" emphasize about the character/attributes of God and why is this important to the children of Israel? _____

_____

10. How long is this term to be used by the children of Israel (Exo. 3:15)? _____

_____

11. What is the 3rd of the 10 commandments (Exo. 20:7)? _____

_____

Thought Question:
Why has the pronunciation of the term YHWH been lost? _____

_____

_____

I AM

I AM

1. What is the purpose of the gospel of John (John 20:30-31)? _____
_____

Throughout his Gospel, John tells us of the claims Jesus made and the reaction of the people to those claims as well as the signs/evidence to substantiate the claims. These claims help develop our concept of the character and attributes of the "Son of God" so our belief in Jesus has meaning and substance. Many claims of Jesus in John's Gospel begin with the words "I AM." This term connects Him with the YHWH of the Old Testament which defines the various aspects of His character and attributes. As these claims are examined, the meaning of the claim, the reaction of the people, and the evidence showing each claim to be true will be emphasized.

Note: all of the "I AM" statements of Jesus in this series of lessons are in the present tense—Jesus IS... We do not serve a Savior who "was" or "will be," but One who "is."

2. What promise does Jesus make (John 8:51)? _____
_____

3. What great men in Jewish history are dead (John 8:52)? _____
_____

The Jews rightly concluded that if Jesus could fulfill His promise (no death for those who kept His words), then Jesus was claiming to have power/authority over death. Neither Abraham nor the prophets possessed this power as evidenced by their deaths.

4. Who would Jesus have to be in order to have authority over death (John 8:53)?
_____
_____

5. Rather than Jesus taking this honor/authority on Himself, who gives Him this honor (John 8:54-55)? _____
_____

6. What does Abraham see (John 8:56)? _____
_____

A. How is this possible? _____
_____

7. The Jews ask a good question. How old would Jesus need to be in order to have
seen Abraham (John 8:57)? _____
_____

8. What is Jesus' answer (John 8:58)? _____
_____

A. How old does this make Jesus? _____
_____

B. What is the connection with Exodus 3:14? _____
_____

9. How do the Jews who heard this claim react and why (John 8:59)? _____
_____

10. Put this claim of Jesus, "I AM," in your own words. _____
_____
_____

11. How does this truth help form your concept of Jesus as the Son of God? _____
_____
_____

I AM
HE (THE MESSIAH)

In Exodus 30:22-33, God gave the children of Israel instructions for making "holy anointing oil." This oil is used to anoint the tabernacle, all its furniture, Aaron the high priest and his sons. Throughout the history of Israel, God selects men to be anointed: kings like David (1 Sam. 16:12-13) and Solomon (1 Kings 1:39) and prophets like Elisha (1 Kings 19:16). This anointing process visibly declares the approval of God. These "anointed ones" are set apart for the function He defined.

The noun "anointed one" is "mashach" (Messiah) in Hebrew and "christos" (Christ) in Greek.

Prophets like Isaiah prophesied of the Messiah, who would come to establish His kingdom and save the world from sin. This Messiah would be Prophet, High Priest, and King. In Luke 4:16-21, Jesus claims to fulfill the prophecy of the Messiah spoken of in Isaiah 61:1-2. He is "anointed" by God to preach, heal and set at liberty those held captive by Satan.

Many times we refer to Jesus of Nazareth as Jesus Christ. Jesus is not His first name and Christ His last name. Both are descriptions of who He is: Jesus = Savior and Christ = the Anointed One.

John's Testimony

1. According to John the baptizer, what is Jesus' God given job (John 1:29-34)? _____
   _____
   _____

2. Upon what basis does John believe these facts about Jesus to be true (John 1:30-34)? _____
   _____

3. At His baptism, with what does God anoint Jesus (Acts 10:37-38)? _____
   _____

A. How does the Father audibly confirm His selection of Jesus as His Messiah (Luke 3:21-22)? _____

_____

4. When Jesus began His ministry in the synagogue in Nazareth, He read from Isaiah 61:1-2. What is He "anointed" by the Spirit to do (Luke 4:16-21)? _____

_____

Jesus in Samaria

5. In the beginning of John 4, Jesus speaks to a woman of Samaria. What does she come to believe about Jesus? Why (John 4:15-19)? _____

_____

_____

6. After asking Jesus a question about worship, of whom does the woman ask (John 4:25)? _____

_____

A. What does she say the Messiah would be able to do? _____

_____

7. What claim does Jesus make (John 4:26)? _____

_____

8. When the woman went into the city to tell of Jesus, what does she say He did (John 4:29)? _____

_____

9. After speaking with Jesus themselves, what do the Samaritans come to believe about Jesus (John 4:42)? _____

_____

10. Put this claim of Jesus, "I am He", in your own words. _____

_____

_____

_____

11. How does this truth help form your concept of Jesus as the Son of God? _____

_____

_____

_____

I AM

THE BREAD OF LIFE

As we have learned, Jesus is "I AM." This truth is simple, yet profound. What does "I AM" mean practically? As we continue to examine the "I AM"s of Jesus, we allow Him to define the multifaceted nature of the Son of God.

"Bread" is a staple of life. Men and women all over the world and at every time in history have eaten bread. With it we are nourished and with that nourishment, we live each day. During the wilderness wandering, God used real bread to teach the children of Israel to trust in Him for their daily spiritual nourishment. "...that He might make you know that man shall not live by bread alone; but man lives by every word that proceeds from the mouth of the LORD," (Deut. 8:3). After feeding the 5,000 with real bread, Jesus, the LORD, made the same spiritual connection when He claimed, "I am the bread of life."

Jesus gives us nourishment for spiritual life. Our initial rebirth comes through His blood, but sustained life comes from reading, digesting and using the nourishment from the teaching of Jesus. He is our "Bread."

1. What miracle does Jesus perform (John 6:5-13)? _____

   _____

   A. How do the people react to the miracle (John 6:14)? _____

   _____

   _____

2. What do the Jews ask Jesus to perform and why (John 6:30-31)? _____

   _____

   A. What is the connection with the miracle Jesus had performed the day before?

   _____

   _____

3. Who actually gave the manna from Heaven, Moses or God (John 6:32)? _____

   _____

4. How does Jesus describe the "bread of God?" Is it a thing or a person (John 6:33)?

_____

_____

5. What claim does Jesus make (John 6:35)? _____

_____

6. What is the promise connected to Jesus' claim of being the "bread of life" (John 6:35)? _____

_____

    A. What contrast is Jesus making with the manna that came from heaven in Moses' time? _____

_____

_____

7. What promise is connected with the claim of Jesus (John 6:39-40)? _____

_____

8. Why do the Jews have difficulty understanding the claim of Jesus (John 6:41-42)?

_____

_____

9. What contrast does Jesus make between the manna coming from heaven in the time of Moses and Himself being the living bread (John 6:48-51)? _____

_____

    A. What is the definition of "eternal life" (John 17:3)? _____

_____

10. Is Jesus referring to His physical body (John 6:52-58)? _____

_____

11. Later when Jesus spoke with His disciples, He further explains this concept of the bread of life. What does He say would bring life (John 6:63)? _____

_____

12. Put this claim of Jesus, "I am the bread of life", in your own words. _____

_____

_____

_____

13. How does this truth help form your concept of Jesus as the Son of God? _____

_____

_____

_____

I AM

THE LIGHT OF THE WORLD

"Let there be light" was the first command on the first day of creation (Gen. 1:3). Light is essential to life on the earth. In places where light is scarce such as caves and the depths of the sea, life is scarce. Mankind lives and thrives when light shines on the earth but sleeps when it is dark. Light brings an understanding of our surroundings, perspective, and the ability to see the right path as well as the dangers. Jesus uses the physical to elevate our eyes to the spiritual quality He possesses. Jesus does not simply show us the light or bring light with Him. He is "the Light of the world."

While Jesus was in Jerusalem celebrating the Feast of the Tabernacles (John 7-9), he made the claim to be the "Light of the world" (John 8:12). The reaction of the Pharisees (8:13) along with "those Jews who believed" (8:31) leads Jesus to make the extraordinary claim to be "I AM" (8:58). The hearers react by taking up stones to kill him for blasphemy. Jesus does not allow the hot opposition to settle before He proves his claims by giving both physical and spiritual light to a man born blind.

1. What promise does Jesus attach to His claim of being the "light of the world" (John 8:12)? _____

_____

   A. What claim is made about Jesus (John 1:4)? _____

   _____

"Light" is an important concept in the book of John. The term is found 24 times in John 1-12. It is always used in the metaphoric sense. The term "darkness" occurs 5 times.

2. What does Jesus see (John 9:1)? _____

_____

3. Why is this man born blind (John 9:2-3)? _____

_____

_____

4. What connection does Jesus make between healing this blind man and His claim of being the "light of the world" (John 9:4-5)? _____

_____

5. What is the process Jesus uses to heal this man (John 9:6-7)? _____
_____

6. What does the blind man believe about Jesus? (Note his growth in faith.)

   · John 9:12 - _____
   _____

   · John 9:17 - _____
   _____

   · John 9:25 - _____
   _____

   · John 9:30 - _____
   _____

   · John 9:35-38 - _____
   _____

7. Why does Jesus come to the world (John 9:39)? _____
_____

8. What is the spiritual condition of the Pharisees (John 9:40-41)? _____
_____

9. What claim is made about Jesus (John 1:4)? _____
_____

10. What can we learn about the contrast between "light" and "darkness" (John 3:19-
    21)? _____
    _____

11. What promise does Jesus make (John 12:36)? _____
_____

12. Put this claim of Jesus, "I am the light of the world," in your own words. _____
    _____
    _____

13. How does this truth help form your concept of Jesus as the Son of God? _____
    _____
    _____

I AM
THE DOOR OF THE SHEEP,
THE GOOD SHEPHERD

Some have called the land of Palestine the "land of shepherds." In John 10, Jesus is in Jerusalem which was within a section of Judea called the Central Plateau. It stretches from Bethel to Hebron for a distance of about 35 miles and varies in width from 14 to 17 miles. Because this land was dry, rough and rocky, it is more pastoral than agricultural.

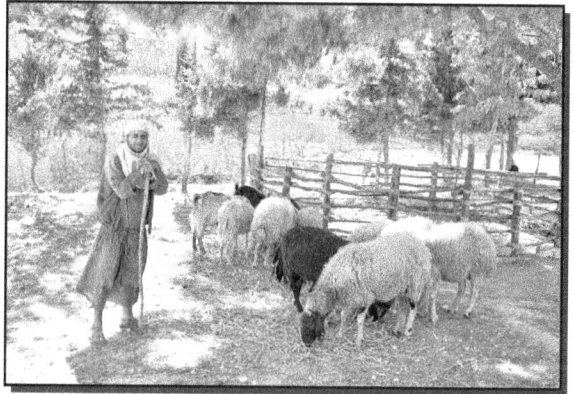

The life of a shepherd is hard, nomadic and solitary. He spends long stretches of time away from his family. He keeps on the move to find food and water. Wild animals such as wolves and bears are a danger for the shepherd and sheep alike. Thieves are also a constant threat.

The shepherd's tools consists of: a scrip—a bag made of skin which contained food, a sling—an offensive and defensive weapon, a staff—a short wooden club studded with nails to ward off beasts and robbers, and a rod—like a shepherd's crook, used to pull back straying sheep.

Sheep are not very smart animals. If left alone, they will die. They are very dependent on the shepherd for their food, water and shelter.

1. What is the contrast between the thief/robber and the shepherd of the sheep in John 10:1-2? _____

_____

2. What are the qualities of the sheep mentioned by Jesus (John 10:3-5)? _____

_____

   A. According to John 10:6, the listeners of Jesus do not understand Jesus' illustration. What is Jesus' point(s)? _____

_____

I am the Door

3. What does Jesus claim to be (John 10:7)? _____
_____

Jesus is not talking about a door to a house. In the cold weather, the shepherd took his sheep into a village where he could find a pen for his sheep and an inn for himself. In warmer weather, he could stay out in the hills searching for pastures. At night, a wall would be made from rock and branches with one opening. This enclosure would keep the sheep from wandering off during the night as well as keep out animals and thieves. The shepherd would lead each sheep through the opening inspecting each as it entered. When all were safely inside, the shepherd would lie down in the opening. Nothing could come in or go out except through him. He literally became "the door."

4. What/who is the "door of the sheep" in Jesus' figure? _____
_____

5. What blessing is attached to entering by the door (John 10:9)? _____
_____

I am the Good Shepherd

6. What is the contrast between the intentions of the thief and the intentions of Jesus (John 10:10)? _____
_____

7. What is the contrast between the hireling and the "good shepherd" (John 10:11-13)? _____
_____

When the temperature dropped, the shepherd would come into town for the night to obtain warmth for himself and the sheep. All the shepherds would put their sheep in a common pen and hire someone to watch them through the night. In the morning, the sheep would be separated. A stranger would have difficulty separating the sheep since they were not branded as cattle (sheep were raised for their wool not their meat). The sheep would separate themselves when they heard their own shepherd's voice calling them. The shepherd knew each sheep by name.

8. Who are the "other sheep" Jesus spoke of and when do they become "one flock" (John 10:16; Eph. 2:13-22)? _____

_____

9. What does Jesus say He had the power to do (John 10:17-18)? _____

_____

   A. If this is true, why does Jesus pray, "Father, if it is possible, let this cup pass from Me; nevertheless, not as I will but as You will," (Matt. 26:36)? _____

   _____

10. What is the reaction of those who heard these claims of Jesus (John 10:19-21)?

_____

11. Put this claim of Jesus, "I am the Door of the sheep. I am the good Shepherd," in your own words. _____

_____

_____

_____

12. How does this truth help form your concept of Jesus as the Son of God? _____

_____

_____

_____

Read Psalms 23 with Jesus in mind.

> *1 The LORD is my shepherd; I shall not want.*
>
> *2 He makes me to lie down in green pastures;*
> *He leads me beside the still waters.*
>
> *3 He restores my soul; He leads me in the paths of righteousness*
> *For His name's sake.*
>
> *4 Yea, though I walk through the valley of the shadow of death,*
> *I will fear no evil; For You are with me;*
> *Your rod and Your staff, they comfort me.*
>
> *5 You prepare a table before me in the presence of my enemies;*
> *You anoint my head with oil; My cup runs over.*
>
> *6 Surely goodness and mercy shall follow me All the days of my life;*
> *And I will dwell in the house of the LORD Forever.*

I AM

THE RESURRECTION AND THE LIFE

What man has power over death? We marvel at the power of modern medicine over many diseases. It is the result of the efforts of many of the best and brightest people. Its power pushes the time of death forward for some but, after centuries of effort, has no power over death. Have you passed by a grave yard lately?

Jesus puts Himself in a category above any man with His claim to be "the Resurrection and the Life." In fact, He puts himself into the category of the great "I AM." Peter said, "it was not possible that He should be held by it (death)" in Acts 2:24.

Normally when we think of the "resurrection" or "life," we think of an event or a belief, but Jesus says "the Resurrection and the Life" is a person.

1. What is Jesus' reaction when He hears Lazarus is sick (John 11:4)? _____
   _____

2. How long does Jesus stay where He is after He hears about Lazarus being sick? Why (John 11:6)? _____
   _____

3. What does Jesus know about Lazarus (John 11:11-15)? _____
   _____

4. How long has Lazarus been dead when Jesus arrives (John 11:17)? _____
   _____

5. What does Martha believe about Jesus (John 11:21-24)? _____

_____

    A. Who else believes the same (John 11:32, 37)? _____

    _____

6. In John 11:22, Martha states her belief that God would give Jesus anything
He asks. She believes God is working through Jesus. What claim does Jesus
make for Himself in John 11:25 that demands Martha raise her understanding of
who Jesus "is?" _____

_____

7. What does Jesus mean when He said, "He who believes in Me, though he may
die, he shall live" (John 11:25)? _____

_____

8. What does Jesus mean when He says, "And whoever lives and believes in Me shall
never die" (John 11:26)? _____

_____

9. What is Martha's reaction to Jesus' claim (John 11:27)? _____

_____

10. What does Jesus do to dead Lazarus (John 11:38-44)? _____

_____

11. What is the reaction of the Jews (John 11:45)? _____

_____

12. What is the reaction of the chief priests and Pharisees (John 11:46-53)? _____

_____

13. Put this claim of Jesus, "I am the resurrection and the life," in your own words.

_____

_____

_____

14. How does this truth help form your concept of Jesus as the Son of God? _____

_____

_____

_____

I AM

TEACHER AND LORD

The roads of the first century were often dusty and dirty. People wore sandals which were soles of leather tied to the bottom of the foot with a few straps. With the perspiration of walking, feet would get dirty and, out of courtesy to the guest (and perhaps the home owner's floor), a basin of water would be kept at the door. As a guest entered, a servant would wash and dry his feet.

On the night before the death of Jesus, He and His apostles gather to eat the Passover meal. The apostles enter the room and talk among themselves, but apparently no servant is present to wash their feet. During the eating of the meal, Jesus purposefully stops and washes the apostles' feet.

This example illustrates how Jesus is the master teacher. Jesus possesses greater authority than any man on the planet yet; He washes His followers feet. Jesus does not only tell us what to do; He shows us who to be.

1. When do the events of John 13 take place (John 13:1)? _____
   _____

   A. Since Jesus knew he would die a terrible, painful death the following day, what would you expect Him to do the evening before? _____
   _____

2. What does Jesus do for the disciples (John 13:3-5)? _____
   _____

3. What is Peter's reaction to what Jesus does (John 13:6-9)? _____
   _____

4. What role does Jesus claim for himself (John 13:12-13)? _____
   _____

   A. What is inferred about the authority of His claim? _____
   _____

Teacher

"Teacher" (Master in KJV) is used 58 times in the New Testament. In John 1:38, John makes it equivalent to the Hebrew word "Rabbi." It is not used exclusively of Jesus. For example, Nicodemus calls Jesus "Teacher from God" in John 3:2 and Jesus calls Nicodemus "teacher of Israel" in John 3:10. The role of a "teacher" in Jewish society is a place of honor. Knowledge of the commandments of God and the ability to teach them are important. By the time of Christ, the people would compete for the position of a rabbi within the synagogues. Prominent rabbis would establish schools in which students paid to learn. A rabbi would develop traditions, and the level of respect for the rabbi determined their acceptance. The rabbi is seen as one who has mastered the material he is teaching. A disciple is not only to learn what the rabbi taught but is to become who he is.

5. As Teacher, what is the lesson Jesus teaches (John 13:14-15)? _____
_____

   A. What does this teach us about being a teacher? _____
_____

Lord

"Lord" (Master) is used 748 times in the New Testament. People did not exclusively use the term only of Jesus. For example, Philip is called "Sir (master)" in John 12:21 and also the supposed gardener in John 20:15. To be a master is not necessarily a religious position. People might call a landowner or business owner "master" as well.

6. As Lord, what is the lesson Jesus exemplifies (John 13:16-17)? _____
_____

7. What evidence does Jesus give that "I am He" (John 13:18-19)? _____
_____

Teacher and Lord

8. As Teacher and Lord, what lesson does Jesus teach (John 13:34-35)? _____
_____

9. Put this claim of Jesus, "I am Teacher and Lord," in your own words. _____
_____
_____
_____

10. How does this truth help form your concept of Jesus as the Son of God? _____
_____
_____
_____

I AM
THE WAY, THE TRUTH, THE LIFE

John records more of Jesus' conversation with His apostles the night before His death than any other gospel writer (John 13-17). In John 13, after washing their feet, Jesus announces Judas would betray Him. He tells them He is leaving and they could not follow Him now but would follow Him afterward. Peter speaks up saying he will follow Jesus to the death, but Jesus foretells Peter's denials. How their heads must have been spinning with confusion and apprehension!

Jesus perceives their hearts are troubled (John 14:1). He makes a promise to them. Far from abandoning them, He is leaving with a purpose. He promises to go and prepare a dwelling place in His Father's house for them. He promises to return and take them to this home with the Father.

Who can make such a claim? To presume not only to have access to the dwelling place of God but to have the authority to expand it and take His followers with him to live in God's home is beyond a mere man.

1. What does Jesus tell His disciples about where He is going (John 14:4)? _____
   _____

2. Does Thomas know where Jesus is going (John 14:5) _____
   _____

3. To whom does Jesus want His disciples to go (John 14:6)? _____
   _____

4. What does Jesus mean when He says, "I am the way" (John 14:6)? (Consider: the word "way" is found 8 times in the gospel of John.) _____
   _____

   A. Why is this claim important to the disciples (and us)? _____
      _____

B. This phrase "the Way" is used several times in Acts. What does it come to mean (Acts 9:2; 16:17; 19:9, 23; 22:4; 24:14, 22)? _____

5. What does Jesus mean when He says, "I am...the truth?" (Consider: the word "truth" is found 26 times in the gospel of John.) _____

A. Why is this claim important to the disciples (and us)? _____

B. What has come through Jesus (John 1:14,17)? _____

C. What comes through the truth (John 8:31-32)? _____

D. What contrast is made between the Devil and Jesus (John 8:44-45)? _____

6. What does Jesus mean when He says, "I am...the life?" (Consider: the word "life" is found 47 times in the gospel of John.) _____

A. Why is this claim important to the disciples (and us)? _____

B. How could Jesus make this claim the night before His death? _____

C. What is the definition of "eternal life" (John 17:3)? _____

D. What connection does John make between Jesus and life in 1 John 5:1-12? _____

E. Does this "life" only refer to our life in Heaven (Gal. 2:20)? _____

7. Put this claim of Jesus, "I am the way, and the truth, and the life," in your own words. _____

8. How does this truth help form your concept of Jesus as the Son of God? _____

I AM
IN THE FATHER

Unfortunately, some create their own Jesus in their minds. Their concept of Jesus is vague. Jesus demands a more concrete, objective understanding of His humanity and divinity. He clearly defines the multifaceted quality of His divinity with these challenging claims.

In fact, Jesus adds detail to our understanding of God in general. Many terms are used in the Old Testament to refer to God: Almighty God, LORD God, I AM, LORD of Hosts among others, but Jesus gives these terms a deeper meaning.

The concept of God being our "Father" appears in the Old Testament but is not developed fully until Jesus becomes flesh and uses this term repeatedly. The term "father" occurs 756 times in the Old Testament. Only seven times does it refer to God as the Father and once to Jesus as the "Everlasting Father" (Isa. 9:6). The term occurs 396 times in the New Testament including 133 times in the gospel of John. Only ten times does "father" refer to an earthly father. 123 times the term refers to God as "Father." The majority of the times the term is used by Jesus to refer to His relationship with "the Father" and a few times to refer to man's relationship with "the Father."

It is noteworthy that the concept of God as "Father" is not found in Buddhism, Hinduism, Taoism or Islam. The true God, however, cannot be understood fully without this concept of an intimate, authoritative relationship.

Jesus' Hometown

1. When Philip encourages Nathanael to investigate Jesus, why is he not initially impressed (John 1:45-46)? _____
_____

   A. After a short conversation, what is Nathanael's conclusion (John 1:47-50)? ___
   _____

Son of Man/Son of God

2. Jesus makes a claim for Himself seeming to draw from the event in Gen. 28:12 where Jacob sees a ladder set on the earth reaching to Heaven. How could Jesus of Nazareth be this ladder (John 1:51)? _____
_____

Jesus' Connection with the Father

3. What relationship does Jesus have with the Father (John 10:37-38)? _____
_____

   A. What proof does Jesus offer for this claim (John 10:25; 5:36)? _____
   _____

4. How is it possible to see the Father when we see Jesus (John 14:7)? _____
_____

5. What claim does Jesus want His apostles to believe (John 14:10-11)? _____
_____

   A. What proof does Jesus offer for this claim? _____
   _____

6. Jesus speaks of the fact His apostles would soon see Him die and be raised from the dead. This resurrection is evidence Jesus is indeed in the Father. Who else is connected to Jesus (John 14:19-20)? _____
_____

7. Just before Jesus goes to the garden of Gethsemane and is betrayed by Judas, He prays with His apostles. He prays for them and "for those who will believe in Me through their word." What does Jesus want all believers to be (John 17:21-23)? __
_____

   A. Why does Jesus want us to be united in this way? _____
   _____

8. Put this claim of Jesus, "I am in the Father," in your own words. _____
_____
_____
_____

9. How does this truth help form your concept of Jesus as the Son of God? _____
_____
_____

I AM
THE TRUE VINE

The cultivation of the grape vine is a part of Jewish life throughout Bible times. Unlike cutting down a crop like wheat each season, the cultivated grape vine produces fruit year after year. Painstaking effort is needed to produce quality fruit. Typically, for the first three years, vines produce no fruit. Racks suspend the vines so the fruit does not touch the ground. Pruning is an annual event done to keep the nourishment concentrated in the fruit. The grape is used as a source of food, but more importantly, to make a beverage to add flavor to and kill the germs in the groundwater. It is a life-source to the people of the land.

God uses the figure of the vine to teach Israel some valuable spiritual lessons. Jesus uses this figure to help us understand our relationship with Him and His relationship with us. Specifically, in John 15, Jesus is preparing His apostles for His return to Heaven and their responsibility to continue His work. The connection between Jesus and His apostles/disciples is crucial for fruit to be produced.

Old Testament Metaphor

1. During the time of Asaph (a contemporary of David, ca 1,000 BC), Asaph pleads with God for His favor to return to Israel. He uses the figure of the vine. Who is the "vine" and what is the point of the figure (Psa. 80:7-18)? _____
   _____

2. During the time of Isaiah (ca 740 BC), Isaiah illustrates the relationship of God ("my Well-beloved") and Israel ("a vineyard"). What is the point of the figure (Isa. 5:1-7)?
   _____
   _____

New Testament Metaphor

3. Jesus uses the figure of a "vineyard" in His teaching ("vineyard" is found 22 times in Matthew—Luke). John only records Jesus using the term "vineyard" or "vine" in chapter 15 of his gospel.

Please identify the following from John 15:

    A. "vine" - _____

    B. "vinedresser" - _____

    C. "branch" - _____

    D. "fruit" - _____

    E. "fire" - _____

4. What is the job of the "vinedresser" (John 15:2)? _____
_____

5. What makes them "clean" (John 15:3)? What does it mean to be "clean?" _____
_____
_____

6. What is the relationship of the vine and the branches (John 15:4)? _____
_____

7. What is the benefit to the branch if it abides in the vine (John 15:5-6)? _____
_____

8. What blessing is given to the branches who abide in the vine (John 15:7)? _____
_____

9. What is the main purpose of the branch (John 15:8)? _____
_____

    A. List passages describing the "fruit" a Christian is to produce? _____
    _____

10. What is the connection between abiding in the love of God and keeping His commandments (John 15:9-10)? _____
_____

11. What will be the result of a proper relationship between the vine and branches
(John 15:11)? _____
_____

12. Put this claim of Jesus, "I am the true vine," in your own words. _____
_____
_____

13. How does this truth help form your concept of Jesus as the Son of God? _____
_____
_____

I AM
A KING

After the sin of Adam and Eve, God began to slowly, yet methodically, reveal His plan to save man from sin's consequences. God's promise that the "Seed of woman" would crush the head of Satan gives the first glimpse of the Messiah (Gen. 3:15). The Seed's victory over Satan would be redemption for man. Later, God reveals more details of His plan when He promises Abraham, "In your seed all the nations of the earth shall be blessed," (Gen. 22:18). The Seed of Abraham would bring great blessings to all the world. Later, God reveals more details of His plan when He promises David, "I will set up your seed after you,...And your house and your kingdom shall be established forever," (2 Sam. 7:12-16). The Seed of David would be a King with an eternal kingdom. Jesus is, in fact, the fulfillment of all these expectations.

Prophecy and Expectation

1. What is prophesied about the kingdom of the Messiah (Isa. 2:2-4)? _____
_____

2. What is prophesied about this kingdom (Dan. 2:44-45)? _____
_____

3. What summary is given of John's preaching (Matt. 3:2)? _____
_____

4. What summary is given of Jesus' preaching (Matt. 4:17)? _____
_____

Jesus' Destiny

5. When Jesus is on trial before Pilate, what question does Pilate ask (John 18:33)?
_____

6. What is the initial answer of Jesus (John 18:34)? (Consider: why does he answer in this way?) _____
_____

7. How does Jesus describe His kingdom (John 18:36)? _____
_____
_____

    A. How is Jesus' description of His kingdom in harmony with the promises and
    prophecies? _____
    _____

8. Does Jesus claim to be a "king" (John 18:37)? _____
_____

    A. What evidence confirms Jesus is born to be king (Luke 1:31-35; Matt. 2:2-6;
    Acts 2:30-31)? _____
    _____

9. What does Pilate have written on the cross of Jesus (John 19:19)? Why? _____
_____

10. What is the reaction of the Jews to what Pilate writes (John 19:20-21)? _____
_____

11. For consideration. Why does Pilate not change what was written on the sign (John
19:22)? _____
_____

12. Put this claim of Jesus, "I am a King," in your own words. _____
_____
_____

13. How does this truth help form your concept of Jesus as the Son of God? _____
_____
_____

I AM
REVIEW

Throughout the Old Testament times, God reveals Himself to man. Through His interaction with man recorded in the Scripture, God defines His divine attributes. By the time of Christ, the man of faith could have a profound appreciation for what it means to be "God."

When the "Word became flesh and dwelt among us" (John 1:14), He is correctly called the "Son of God" and the "Son of man." Jesus is human, which qualifies Him to be High Priest, Mediator, Author, Advocate and the perfect sacrifice for sin. Jesus is also divine, which qualifies Him to fulfill these same roles. With the "I am" claims in the book of John, Jesus directly identifies Himself with what man knew about God. In fact, Jesus is the fullest revelation of God ever given. These "I am" claims of Jesus not only show He is the Son of God but help us understand who God is in a complete way.

In this last lesson, we would like to review the claims of Jesus by making direct connections with the known qualities of God in the Old Testament.

1. Please examine the following references from the Old Testament Scriptures and record:
   A. The quality of God exhibited in each context.
   B. How the quality is beyond human capability.
   C. Which of the "I AM" claims of Jesus exhibits the same quality.
   The point is to connect the qualities that are uniquely God's as illustrated in the Old Testament that are possessed by Jesus. In fact, notice how Jesus gives us an even fuller definition of these divine qualities.

A. Gen. 2:7 _____

_____

_____

B. Ex. 3:14-15 _____

_____

_____

C. Ex. 13:21 _____
_____
_____

D. Deut. 8:3 _____
_____
_____

E. Deut. 30:19-20 _____
_____
_____

F. Joshua 3:9-13 _____
_____
_____

G. 1 Sam. 8:7 _____
_____
_____

H. Psa. 18:28 _____
_____
_____

I. Psa. 23 _____
_____
_____

J. Isa. 2:5 _____
_____
_____

K. Isa. 5:1-2, 7 _____
_____
_____

L. Malachi 1:14 _____
_____
_____

2. Please examine the following Old Testament Messianic prophecies. Record which of the "I AM" claims of Jesus fulfills the prophecy.

A. Psa. 2:2 _____
_____
_____

B. Psa. 2:6-9 _____
_____
_____

C. Psa. 110 _____
_____
_____

D. Isa. 2:3 _____
_____
_____

E. Isa. 60:1-3, 19-20 _____
_____
_____

F. Isa. 61:1,2 _____
_____
_____

G. Jer. 31:10 _____
_____
_____

H. Ez. 34:23-31 _____
_____
_____

I. Ez. 37:21-24 _____
_____
_____

J. Micah 5:2 _____
_____
_____

Regarding the preparation of this material, the author is indebted to the works of the following individuals:

Hailey, Homer. That You May Believe. Grand Rapids, MI: Baker Book House, 1973.

Wiersbe, Warren W. Jesus in the Present Tense. Colo9rado Springs, CO: David Cook, 2011.

Hendriksen, William. New Testament Commentary, Exposition of the Gospel According to John. Grand Rapids, MI: Baker Book House, 1953.

www.ingramcontent.com/pod-product-compliance
Lightning Source LLC
Chambersburg PA
CBHW081252040426

42452CB00015B/2794